Stories and Parables *for* Preachers and Teachers

Fr. Paul Wharton

Paulist Press • New York • Mahwah

Dedicated with love

to my parents
and brothers and sisters:
my first storytellers

Library of Congress
Catalog Card Number: 86-60140

ISBN: 0-8091-2796-2

Published by Paulist Press
997 Macarthur Boulevard
Mahwah, New Jersey 07430

Printed and bound in the
United States of America

Contents

OBSTACLES ALONG THE WAY

DESTINY AND THE WAY

Introduction

In every age, men [*and women*] *have set out on pilgrimages, spiritual journeys, on personal quests. Driven by pain, drawn by longing, lifted by hope, singly and in groups, they come in search of relief, enlightenment, peace, power, joy, or they know not what.*

*Sheldon Kopp**

And in every age, men and women have told stories to help themselves and guide others along these journeys. The image of the human life as a journey is both ancient and new, having received a rediscovered emphasis in recent years. People tell stories to provide meaning and understanding for life and existence. People tell stories to put the listeners and narrators in touch with the mystery of God, the mystery of the world, and the mystery of humanity. When asked who we are, we tell our own stories.

If, as Elie Wiesel suggested, God created people because God loves stories and so much of Jesus' preaching was in parables, then more attention ought to be given this wonderful literary form. Stories can capture the imagination, challenge, enlighten, provoke, instill values or deeply disturb people. Stories can put us in touch with God and ourselves. They are ideally suited for teaching, preaching, personal reflection, and prayer.

Of all the homilies and talks that I have heard over the years, the ones that were most meaningful and longest re-

---

*Sheldon B. Kopp, *If You Meet the Buddha on the Road, Kill Him* (New York: A Bantam Book published by arrangement with Behavior and Science Books, Inc., © 1972), p. 3.

membered were the ones with an appropriate story. As a preacher, I am told again and again how certain stories have deeply affected people and prodded them along their own spiritual journeys. Over the years I have collected stories that have touched me and others, and I present some of them in this book in the hope that they may touch still others as well.

Biblical scholars tell us that the interpretations found after some of Jesus' parables in the Gospels were added later by the early Church or the evangelists. A good story speaks for itself and ought never be chained down to one meaning or interpretation. I have tried to avoid this where possible since a good story will say different things to different people at different times. In the interests of organizing the stories in this collection they have been titled, but many of the stories can be used in different ways. Another temptation to be avoided is to draw out the meaning of a story *ad nauseam* so that the wonder and mystery is destroyed.

I used several criteria in choosing the stories for this collection. First, they had to somehow address an aspect of the spiritual journey all of us must make back to God. Second, they had to be relatively short. Long stories tend to spend too much time on details so that either the point can be lost or the story itself becomes the object of focus rather than a vehicle for mystery. Finally, they had to somehow provoke the reader or hearer to question and wonder about his or her own journey.

This book has been divided into four sections. "The Way to God" concerns both the call to follow God and the human search for God. The second section describes attitudes and actions Christians are called to have as they journey through life toward God. "Obstacles Along the Way," as the title suggests, includes stories about those attitudes and actions which hinder growth and impede progress in our relationship with God. The final part deals with the goal of the journey: union with God in this world and eternal life in the next.

It is my hope that *Stories and Parables for Preachers and Teachers* will be used by a variety of people for many reasons. Preachers and teachers are certainly encouraged to draw upon these since people like to hear stories. These stories can be used for personal reflection, spiritual direction, or prayer. Parents could use many of them to discuss our faith with their children. With its emphasis on the Christian journey, this book is ideal for those working with catechumens in the Rite of Christian Initiation of Adults. These stories can provide insights in the catechumens' own stories. However you may choose to use these stories, I hope you allow yourself time to reflect on them first.

Speaking from experience, I caution readers to avoid overdosing on these stories. It is tempting to run from story to story without taking time to listen, reflect, and wonder. I recommend reading only one story at a sitting to allow them to speak in all their richness.

Being a passionate collector of parables and stories for preaching, teaching, and reflection, I would appreciate good stories that readers have written, used, or collected. Any and all contributions will be gratefully received. They may be sent to me at 826–32nd Street, Parkersburg, West Virginia 26101.

The Way that can be told of
is not an Unvarying Way . . .
The Way is like an empty vessel
that may yet be drawn from
without ever needing to be filled.
It is bottomless.

Lao Tzu

When the pilgrim of truth
comes on his journey
to the region of the parable,
he finds its interpretation.
It is not a fruit or a jewel to be stored,
but a well springing by the wayside.

George MacDonald

The rarest and mightiest possession
of the human spirit
can be discovered only by means of a story
and by no other process of thinking.

Gordon Chalmers

THE WAY TO GOD

Desire

There was a young man who approached a hermit with this request: "Show me how I can find God." "How great is this desire of yours?" asked the saintly man. "More than anything in the world," came the reply. The hermit took the young man to the shore of a lake and they waded into the water until it was up to their necks. Then the holy man put his hand on the other's head and pushed him under water. The young man struggled desperately, but the hermit did not release him until he was about to drown. When they returned to the shore, the saint asked, "Son, when you were under water, what did you want more than anything in the world?" "Air," he replied without hesitation. "Well, then, when you want to find God as much as you just then wanted air, your eyes will be opened to the wonder of God."

Many Ways

There was a very wise king who had built for himself a strange and wonderful palace. In the center of the palace was a room in which stood the throne. Only one door led into this room. All through the palace were passageways, halls, and corridors that twisted and turned about and led in every direction. When the palace stood finished, the king sent an order to all his people commanding them to come before him. He sat on his throne and waited. The people came to the outside of the palace and stared in wonder at the confusion of corridors. They cried, "There is no way to the king!" But the crown prince, who was standing at the door, pointed inside and said, "Here the king waits for you. All ways lead to him."

Searching

There was a wealthy king who was quite sincere about religious matters and questions. One night, the king was awakened by a fearful stomping on the roof above his bed. Alarmed, he shouted, "Who's there?"

"A friend," came the reply. "I've lost my camel."

The king, angered by such a ridiculous statement, screamed, "You fool! Are you looking for a camel on the roof?"

"You fool!" the voice answered. "Are you looking for God while you wear silk pajamas and lie in a bed made of gold?"

These simple words, we are told, filled the king with terror, and he rose from his sleep to become a very great saint.

Cease Struggling

A drowning boy was struggling in the water. On the shore stood his mother in an agony of fright and grief. By her side stood a strong man, seemingly indifferent to the boy's fate. Again and again did the suffering woman appeal to him to save her boy, but he made no move. Soon the desperate struggles of the boy began to lessen. He was losing strength and presently he arose to the surface weak and helpless. At once the man leaped into the stream and brought the boy to safety. "Why did you not save my boy sooner?" asked the now grateful mother. "Madam, I could not as long as he struggled. He would have dragged us both to certain death. But when he grew weak and ceased to struggle, then it was easy for me to save him."

Prayer Is the Key

A poor, but honest, jeweler was arrested for a crime he never committed. He was placed in a high and well-protected prison in the center of the city. One day, after he had been imprisoned for many months, his wife came to the main gate. She told the guards how her husband, the poor jeweler, was a devout and prayerful man. He would be lost without his simple prayer rug. Would they not allow him to have this single possession? The guards agreed that it would be harmless and gave him the prayer rug. Five times daily he would unroll his rug and pray.

Weeks passed, and one day the jeweler said to his jailers: "I am bored sitting here day after day with nothing to do. I am a good jeweler, and if you will let me have some pieces of metal and some simple tools, I will make you jewelry. You could then sell what I make in the bazaar and add to your low salaries as jailers. I ask for little—just something to fill the idle hours and to keep my skill in practice." The poorly paid jailers agreed that it would be a good arrangement.

Days grew into weeks, weeks into months. One bright morning when the guards came to the jeweler's cell, they found it empty. No sign was found of the prisoner or of how he escaped. Some time later the real criminal was arrested for the crime of which the poor jeweler had been falsely accused. One day in the city's bazaar, long after that, one of the guards saw the ex-prisoner, the jeweler. Quickly explaining that the real criminal had been caught, he asked the jeweler how he had escaped. The jeweler proceeded to tell the amazing story.

His wife had gone to the main architect who had designed the prison. She obtained from him the blueprints of the cell doors and locks. She then had a design woven into a prayer rug. Each day as he would pray, his head would touch the rug. Slowly, he began to see that there was a design, within a design, within another design, and that it was the design of the lock on his cell door. From the bits of leftover metal and his simple tools, he fashioned a key and escaped!

Close to Home

Once upon a time there lived in Cracow, Poland a rabbi named Eisek who dreamed three times that there was a treasure beneath a particular bridge in Prague. After the third dream, Eisek finally walked the long distance to Prague. When he found the bridge, the captain of the soldiers who were guarding asked him why he had come. Eisek told him of his three dreams.

The captain replied that if he had had faith in dreams, he would have gone to Cracow a long time ago when he dreamed that there was a treasure buried in the ground under the stove of a Jew named Eisek. When Rabbi Eisek heard this, he left immediately, walked the long journey home, and dug up the treasure underneath his kitchen stove.

God Is Waiting To Be Found

A Hasidic story tells of a little boy playing hide-and-seek with his friends. For some unknown reason they stopped playing while he was hiding. He began to cry. His old grandfather came out of the house to see what was troubling him and to comfort him. After learning what had happened, the grandfather said, "Do not weep, my child, because the boys did not come to find you. Perhaps you can learn a lesson from this disappointment. All of life is like a game between God and us. Only it is God who is weeping, for we are not playing the game fairly. God is waiting to be found, but many have gone in search of other things."

Answering the Call of Christ

According to an old legend, when the Magi were following the star of Bethlehem, they came to the house of a certain woman. They said to her, "Come with us! We have seen his star in the east and we are going to worship him."

"Oh," she said, "I would love to go. I heard that he would be coming one day and I have been looking forward to it. But I can't come now. I must set my house in order; then I will follow you and find him."

But when her work was done, the wise men were out of sight, the star shone no more in the heavens, and she never saw Jesus.

Look Together

A man had been wandering about in a forest for several days, unable to find his way out. Finally, he saw a man approaching him in the distance. His heart was filled with joy. "Now I shall surely find out which is the right way out of this forest," he thought to himself. When they neared each other, he asked the man, "Brother, will you please tell me the way out of the forest? I have been wandering about in here for several days and I can't find the way out."

The other man said to him, "Brother, I do not know the way out either, for I, too, am lost. But this much I can tell you. Do not go the way I have gone, for I know that it is not the way. Now come, let us search for the way out together."

Respond Now

A young eastern king wished to be good and wise, and to rule his people according to the will of God. He called together the wisest men of his realm and ordered them to gather all the wisdom into books so that he could read and learn for himself how to rule well.

The wise men began their tremendous task, and after thirty years it was finished. A long string of camels bearing five thousand volumes came to the palace. The king, already middle-aged, was occupied with many duties and plans. He looked at the loaded camels and said, "I am too busy to read so many books. Take them away and condense them for me."

The work of condensing took fifteen years, and then the wise men proudly produced five hundred volumes. "Still far too many," said the king. "Fifty ought to be enough." Most of the wise men were dead, but their successors carried on and in ten years they brought fifty books to the king. But by this time the king was old and tired. "You must make a summary of it all into one book." It took them five years, but when they brought the precious volume to the king, it was too late, for he lay on his deathbed.

Finding Grace at the Center

There was a little fish who swam up to his mother one day and said, "Mom, what is this water that I hear so much about?" Laughing, she responded, "You silly little fish. Why, it's around you and within you and gives you life. Just swim to the top of the pond and lie there for a while; then you will find out what water is."

Another time there was a little fawn who walked up to her mother and said, "Mommy, what is this air that I hear so much about?" Smiling, she answered, "You silly little deer. Why, air is within you and around you. Air gives you life. If you want to know what air is, stick your head in the stream and you'll find out."

Finally, there was a certain young man who was beginning his spiritual journey. After having difficulty knowing where to turn, he asked a holy woman, "What is this God I hear so much about?" . . .

So Simple It Is Difficult

There is a story in the Hebrew Scriptures (2 Kings 5:1–19) about a man named Namaan who was infected with leprosy. Seeking to find a cure, he went to visit the prophet Elisha because of the suggestion of a servant girl. Elisha told him that if he wanted to cure himself of this dreaded disease, he should bathe himself seven times in the Jordan River. But Namaan thought that something so simple would never work and he refused. Finally, one of his advisors said,

"Sir, if this prophet had told you to do something really difficult, you would have done so without hesitation. All the more reason you should do something so simple." Namaan gave in, bathed himself seven times, and was cured of his leprosy.

Letting Go

Once upon a time there was an old man from Crete. He loved his land with a deep intensity, so much so that when he perceived he was about to die, he had his sons bring him outside and lay him on his beloved earth. As he was about to expire, he reached down by his side and clutched some earth into his hands.

He now appeared before heaven's gate. God, as an old white-bearded man, came out to greet him: "Welcome. You've been a good man. Please, come into the joys of heaven." But as the old man started to enter the pearly gates, God said, "Please. You must let the soil go." "Never!" said the old man, stepping back. "Never!" And so God departed sadly, leaving the old man outside the gates.

A few eons went by. God came out again, this time as a friend, an old drinking crony. They had a few drinks, told some stories, and then God said, "All right, now it's time to enter heaven, friend. Let's go." And they started for the pearly gates. And once more God requested that the old man let go of the soil and once more he refused.

More eons rolled by. God came out once more, this time as a delightful and playful granddaughter. "Oh granddaddy," she said, "you're so wonderful and we all miss you. Please come inside with me." The old man nodded and she helped him up, for by this time he had indeed grown very old and arthritic. In fact, so arthritic was he that he had to prop up the right hand holding Crete's soil with his left hand They moved toward the pearly gates and at this point his strength quite gave out. His gnarled fingers would no longer stay clenched in a fist with the result that the soil sifted out between them until his hand was empty. He then entered heaven. The first thing he saw was his beloved island.

What We Can Be

Hoping to find a few days' work, a traveling portrait painter stopped at a small town. One of his clients there was the town drunk who, in spite of his dirty, unshaven face and bedraggled clothes, sat for his portrait with all the dignity he could display. After the artist had labored a little longer than usual, he lifted the painting from the easel and presented it to the man. "This isn't me," the astonished drunk slurred as he studied the smiling, well-dressed man in the painting. The artist, who had looked beneath the exterior and seen his inner beauty, thoughtfully replied, "But it's the man you could be."

Conversion

A very poor man lived alone in his little hut. One day a wealthy man came to buy his hut. The poor man decided to sell it and went about the place patching the roof and repairing it carefully, feeling a sense of pride that the rich man should desire his hut. After the money was paid, the new owner began at once to tear down the shack. The poor, bewildered man shouted out to him, "Don't tear down my little home. I have repaired it all so nicely." But the wealthy man replied, "I do not want your shack; I only want the site, the corner lot."

Leap of Faith

One night a house caught fire and a young boy was forced to flee to the roof. The father stood on the ground below with outstretched arms, calling to his son, "Jump! I'll catch you." He knew the boy had to jump to save his life.

However, all the boy could see between himself and his dad was fire, smoke, and blackness. As can be imagined, the child was filled with panic. His father yelled again, "Jump, son! I will catch you." But the boy protested, "Daddy, I can't see you." The father replied, "But I can see you and that is all that matters."

Empty Yourself

There was a university professor who went searching for the meaning of life. After several years and many miles, he came to the hut of a particularly holy hermit and asked to be enlightened. The holy man invited his visitor into his humble dwelling and began to serve him tea. He filled the pilgrim's cup and then kept on pouring so that tea was soon dripping onto the floor. The professor watched the overflow until he could no longer restrain himself. "Stop! It is full. No more will go in." "Like this cup," said the hermit, "you are full of your own opinions, preconceptions, and ideas. How can I teach you unless you first empty your cup?"

Awareness

A Zen student, hoping to become a teacher, studied with the Master for ten years. After his time of apprenticeship, he was ready to become a teacher of Zen. Many years passed and the young teacher decided to visit his old teacher. It was a rainy day, so he left his umbrella and wooden clogs outside. Upon entering the presence of the Master, the latter said, "You left your wooden clogs and umbrella outside, didn't you?" "Yes," replied the young teacher. "Did you place your umbrella to the left or to the right of your clogs?" The young teacher became flushed and confused, for he couldn't remember. As a result of his lack of alertness and awareness, he became a student once again. For the next ten years he again practiced the art of constant awareness.

ATTITUDES AND ACTIONS ALONG THE WAY

Discipleship

A young man was apprenticed to a master artist who produced the most beautiful stained glass windows anywhere. The apprentice could not approach the master's genius, so he borrowed his master's tools, thinking that was the answer. After several weeks, the young man said to his teacher, "I'm not doing any better with your tools than I did with mine." The teacher replied, "So, it's not the *tools* of the master you need; it's the *spirit* of the master you need."

Church

A blind man and a lame man happened to come at the same time to a very bad piece of road. The former begged the latter to guide him through his difficulties. "How can I do that," said the lame man, "as I am scarcely able to drag myself along? But if you were to carry me, I can warn you about anything in the way: my eyes will be your eyes and your feet will be mine." "With all my heart," replied the blind man. "Let us serve one another." So taking his lame companion on his back, they traveled with safety and pleasure.

Church

Once there was a young man who wanted to find God, so he went into a large, beautiful cathedral. He thought that under the spacious domes, in the light of the stained glass windows, and in the presence of the glittering mosaics he might experience God. Filled with feelings of God's closeness, he put his head down on the back of the pew in front of him.

A few minutes later he felt a tapping on his shoulder. Looking up, he saw an old woman. "Are you hungry?" she asked. "I could give you a few dollars to get something to eat." Realizing the risk the woman had taken and the simple love that prompted it, the man thanked her but said that he was all right. A few minutes later he left the church, knowing that he had found God in more than one way.

Evangelize

After Jesus returned to heaven, he and the Archangel Gabriel were talking. Even in heaven Jesus bore the marks of the crucifixion. Gabriel said, "Master, you must have suffered horribly! Do people know and appreciate how you love them and what you did for them?"

Jesus replied, "Oh, no; not yet. Right now only a few people in Palestine know."

Gabriel was perplexed: "Then what have you done to let everyone know about your love?"

Jesus answered, "I have asked Peter, Andrew, James, John, and a few more friends to tell others about me. Those who are told will tell others about me, and yet others still others until the last man and the last woman in the farthest corner of the earth will have heard the story of how I gave my life for them because I love them so much."

Gabriel frowned and looked rather skeptical. "Yes, but what if Peter and the others grow weary? What if the people who come after them forget? Surely you have made other plans?"

Said Jesus, "Gabriel, I haven't made any other plans. I'm counting on them."

Share the Good News

According to an ancient story, there were four men walking through a woods when, suddenly, they came across a high wall. Intrigued, they built a ladder to see what was on the other side. When the first man climbed to the top, he cried in delight. The same thing happened with both the second and the third men. When the fourth man reached the top, he smiled at what he saw: lush, green gardens with fruit trees of every kind, streams teeming with fish, and animals, wild and tame, in abundance. Like the others, he was tempted to jump down. But he then thought of his family, friends, and neighbors and went back to share with them the good news he had discovered.

Holiness

A student of the Torah came to his teacher and announced that, in his opinion, he was qualified for ordination as a rabbi. "What are your qualifications?" asked the sage.

The student replied, "I have disciplined my body so that I can sleep on the ground, eat the grass of the field, and allow myself to be whipped three times a day."

"See that yonder white ass," said the teacher, "and be mindful that it sleeps on the ground, eats the grass of the field, and is whipped no less than three times daily. Up to the present you may qualify to be an ass, but certainly not a rabbi."

Faith

One year a rural community was suffering from a terrible drought and their crops—their livelihood—were threatened. The priest told his flock, "There isn't anything that will save us except a special litany for rain. Go to your homes, fast every day from sunrise to sunset, believe that God will answer our prayers, and come on Sunday for the litany of rain."

The villagers heard him, fasted during the week, and went to church on Sunday morning. But as soon as the priest saw them, he was furious. He said, "Go away! I will not do the rain litany. You do not believe."

"But, Father," they protested, "we fasted and believed."

"Believe? Then where are your umbrellas?"

Faith

A tourist came too close to the edge of the Grand Canyon, lost his footing and plunged over the side, clawing and scratching to save himself. Somehow he was able to grab hold of a small, shrubby bush. Filled with terror, he called out, "Is there anyone up there? Can anyone help me?" He heard a reassuring voice say, "I'm here: the Lord your God."

The man said, "I am so glad you came along. I can't hold on much longer." The Lord said, "Before I help you, I want to know if you believe in me." The man answered, "Lord, I certainly believe in you. I go to church every Sunday, sometimes even on Wednesdays. I read my Bible, pray every day, and even put a few dollars in the collection plate."

The Lord replied, "But do you really believe in me?" The man was getting more desperate. "Lord, you can't believe how much I believe in you. I believe!"

The Lord said, "Good. Now let go of the branch."

The man stammered, "But, Lord . . ."

And the voice of the Lord came back, "If you believe in me, let go of the branch."

The man was silent for a minute and then yelled, "Is there anyone else up there?"

Trust in God

There was a terrible flood somewhere and a clergyman went into the deep waters to help anyone he could. The water was above his waist and still rising as he grabbed an injured man and woman. A rowboat came near and a guy yelled, "Let me save you!" But the preacher said, "Take these two. God will save me!" And so the boat left him.

The water was above the man's chin as he struggled to hold onto a mother and two kids. Another boat came by and a man said, "Here, let me save you." Again, he said, "Save these poor people. God will save me." The boat left with the others.

Finally, the water went over the preacher's head and he

drowned. But he found himself at the pearly gates and Saint Peter ushered him into the presence of the Almighty. The clergyman said, "Lord, I have always lived a good life: feeding the hungry, helping the homeless, praying often, and leading people to faith in you. Tell me, Lord, why didn't you save me when I was in that awful flood?"

God replied, "Don't blame me. I did everything I could to save you. Didn't I send two boats for you?"

Hope

A king, engaged to be married, had to set out on a long journey. Days, months, and years passed without any word from him. His fiancée waited for him sorrowfully, but without abandoning hope for his return.

Some of the girl's companions said with pretended compassion and spiteful glee, "Poor girl, it seems your love has forgotten all about you and will never come back." Upset and heartbroken by these words, the maiden wrapped herself in grief and wept much when she was left alone.

She then picked up the last letter the king had sent her, in which he swore that he would remain ever true and faithful to her. Rereading it, her heart once more became peaceful, her spirits lifted, and she continued to wait patiently for his return.

After many years, the king came home. Amazed, he asked his intended wife, "How was it possible for you to remain faithful to me for so long?" "My king," she answered, "I had your letter and believed you."

Love One Another

There is an ancient tradition about the last days of John the Evangelist. He lived to a great age and became so feeble that he had to be carried to the meetings of the faithful. There, because of his weakness, he was unable to deliver a long discourse; so at each gathering he simply repeated the words: "Little children, love one another." The disciples, weary of hearing the same words over and over, asked him why he never said anything else. And to them, John gave this answer, "Do this alone and it is enough."

Love of Neighbor

It was an ancient rabbi who asked his students how they could tell when night had ended and day was on its way back. "Could it be when you see an animal in the distance and can tell whether it is a sheep or a dog?" "No," answered the rabbi. "Could it be when you look at a tree in the distance and can tell whether it is a fig tree or a peach tree?" "No." "Well, then," the students demanded, "when is it?" "It is when you look on the face of any man or woman and see that she or he is your brother or sister. Because if you cannot do that, then no matter what time it is, it is still night."

Charity

A lady of high rank went out begging on a miserably cold day. She wore ragged clothes, put a shawl on her head, and carried a basket. She wanted to test the charity of her neighbors. At some houses she was given things of absolutely no value; at others she was spurned with harsh words. Only in one place was she received with kindness, and that was at the cottage of a poor man. Here she was taken into a warm room and fed a warm meal.

The next day all the people the lady had visited were unexpectedly invited to the castle, where they were led by servants to the spacious dining hall. Place cards showed each guest where to sit at the table. On the plate before each person was the same thing that person had given the disguised lady the day before. Some plates were completely empty. Only the poor man was served a heaping plate of appetizing food.

Then the countess entered the dining room and explained to the guests, "Yesterday, to test your charity, I went about the village dressed as a beggar. Today I am serving you the same thing you gave me yesterday."

Service

A king questioned every scholar and sage who came to his court, "Which is the best service and which is the best time to render it?" He could get no answer that satisfied him. One day while pursuing the forces of a rival king, he got separated from his army in the thick forest. He rode a long way, exhausted and hungry, until he reached a hermitage. There an old monk received him warmly and offered him a cup of cool water. After taking some rest in the monk's bed, the king asked, "Which is the best service?" The monk said, "Giving a thirsty man a cup of water." And which is the best time to render it?" The answer was, "When he comes far and lonely, looking for some place he can get it."

Give Thanks

A farmer brought a load of wheat to the grain elevator in a nearby town. He stopped at a restaurant and sat down near a group of young fellows who were acting up, shouting at the cook, and heckling the waitress. When his meal was set before him, the old man bowed his head in prayer. One of the smart-alecks thought he would have some fun with the farmer. So he shouted in a voice that could be heard by everyone: "Hey, pop, does everyone do that where you come from?" Calmly, the man turned toward the lad and in an equally loud voice replied, "No, son, the pigs don't."

What Prayer Is Not For

A Navajo, a Hopi, and an Apache were speaking about how powerful their prayers were. The Navajo said, "You know, we Navajos pray for healing, and the patients get well about half the time." The Hopi said, "Well, we Hopis pray for rain and it happens about seventy percent of the time." Finally, the Apache spoke up: "Yes, but we Apaches have the sunrise dance, and it works every time."

Prayer

A young girl was quite fond of her little doll. One day, not watching where she was going, she tripped and fell. When she got up she found that her doll was badly damaged. Her brother, who saw all this, laughed when he saw the broken doll. "Laugh all you want," she told him, "but I am going to pray to God to fix my doll."

"Oh, yeah? He won't even answer you," jeered the brother.

"I'll bet he will," the girl replied with complete conviction.

The girl began to pray and her brother went away to play. When he returned a few hours later there was the doll, still in pieces. "Looks like you lost the bet," he taunted. "God didn't answer you at all."

"Oh yes he did," the girl replied. "God said, 'No.' "

Prayer

Once upon a time a monk was walking down a country road. It was early in the morning, and he was going to meet some good friends who lived a great distance away. He had on his brown robe, his head was tonsured, and his sandals were slapping against the road raising little clouds of dust in the sun.

Around noontime he began to tire. It was time to eat; only he had forgotten to bring a lunch so he began to get edgy, even a little bit paranoid about the length of the road, the heat of the sun, and the "why" of the journey. He was completely uncentered or distracted around 1:30 P.M. when he stumbled across a rock right in the middle of the road.

He hadn't even seen it, so taken up was he with his own thoughts and concerns. With the pain of the wounded toe, however, he immediately became aware of his surroundings.

What was that rock doing there? His mind started off in a new direction. Why would a rock be right in the center of the road *he* was walking on? As though someone had intended it? (The rock began to grow in size.) That's it! Someone had put the rock there just so he would stumble on it! (The rock grew even larger.) Someone who didn't like him (the rock by now had grown so large that it blocked the road entirely). His mind raced with the names of people who didn't like him and perhaps wanted to get even with him.

By this time, the rock had become an insurmountable mountain. The monk sat by the side of the road in the shade of a tree, staring up at the gigantic mountain that had risen up to block his efforts and frustrate his plans.

Along this same road came a lady, and, seeing the distracted monk, she went over to him and asked him what was the matter. He told her the whole story of his desires and good intentions, and how he had been wounded and blocked by the great mountain that someone had put in his way. The lady spent some time with the monk talking with him. Then she went over to the center of the road, picked up the little rock, and threw it aside. To say the least, the monk was surprised! As he left the place of his accident and his fortunate encounter with Lady Prayer, he noticed that the mountain was only a rock after all, hardly big enough to prevent him from making his journey and seeing his friends.

A Vision for the Future

The leader of a certain Indian tribe encamped at the base of a mountain was dying. The chief summoned his three sons and said, "I am dying and one of you must succeed me as the head of our tribe. I want each of you to climb our holy mountain and bring back something beautiful. The one whose gift is the most outstanding will succeed me." After several days the sons returned. The first brought his father a flower which grew near the summit and was extremely rare and beautiful. The second son brought his father a stone which was colorful, smooth, and round, having been polished by rain and sandy winds. The third son's hand was empty.

He said, "Father, I have brought nothing back to show you. As I stood on top of the holy mountain, I saw that on the other side was a beautiful land filled with green pastures and a crystal lake. And I have a vision of where our tribe could go for a better life. I was so overwhelmed by what I saw and by what I was thinking that I could not bring anything back." And the father replied, "You shall be our tribe's new leader, for you have brought back the most precious thing of all—the gift of a vision for a better future."

Combating Evil

The pupils of a Hasidic rabbi approached their spiritual leader with a complaint about the prevalence of evil in the world. Intent upon driving out the forces of darkness, they requested the rabbi to counsel them. The rabbi suggested that they take brooms and attempt to sweep the darkness from a cellar. The bewildered disciples applied themselves to sweeping out darkness, but to no avail. The rabbi then advised his followers to take sticks and to beat vigorously at the darkness to drive out the evil. When this likewise failed, he counseled them to go down again into the cellar and to protest against the darkness by shouting at it. When this, too, failed, he said, "My children, let each of you meet the challenge of darkness by lighting a candle." The disciples descended to the cellar and kindled their lights. They looked, and behold! the darkness had been driven out.

How To Change the World

A wise, old middle-eastern mystic said this about himself. "I was a revolutionary when I was young and all my prayer to God was: 'Lord, give me the energy to change the world.' As I approached middle age and realized that my life was half-gone without my changing a single soul, I changed my prayer to: 'Lord, give me the grace to change all those who come into contact with me. Just my family and friends and I shall be satisfied.' Now that I am an old man and my days are numbered, I have begun to see how foolish I have been. My one prayer now is: 'Lord, give me the grace to change myself.' If I had prayed for this right from the start, I would not have wasted my life."

Gentleness

The wind and the sun once had a quarrel. The wind boasted that he was much stronger than the sun. He said, "I'll show you that I am stronger. See that old man over there with the big coat on? I bet I can make him take off his coat much quicker than you can." "All right," said the sun, "we'll see."

So the sun went behind a cloud, but left a little hole so that he could peep through and see what the wind did. The wind blew and blew as hard as he could, causing a terrible storm; but the harder he blew, the tighter the old man wrapped the coat around himself. In the end, the poor old wind had to become calm and give up.

Then it was the sun's turn. He came out from behind the cloud and smiled with sunshine at the old man. After a while, the old man began to mop his brow, then he pulled off his coat. So the sun beat the wind.

Co-Partner with God

Once there was a king who invited his subjects to a banquet. He told each guest to bring a flask of wine and informed each that his wine would be poured into a large wine vat. Each one thought, "What will my small flask of wine mean? I will bring my small flask of water and no one will know the difference." When the guests were assembled at the banquet, the king summoned his servants to serve the guests with the contents of the vat. Each was served water, for they all had thought, "What will my small flask of wine mean? I will bring a flask of water instead and no one will know the difference."

Building for the Future

Once there was a good man who wanted to do good. One day he noticed the miserable conditions in which a poor carpenter lived. The rich man called the carpenter in and commissioned him to build a beautiful house. "I want this to be an ideal cottage. Use only the best materials, employ only the best workmen, and spare no expense." He said that he was going on a journey and that he hoped the house would be finished when he returned.

The carpenter saw this as his great opportunity. Therefore, he skimped on materials, hired inferior workers at low wages, covered their mistakes with paint and cut corners wherever he could. When the rich man returned, the carpenter brought him the key and said, "I have followed your instructions and built your house as you told me to." "I'm glad," said the rich man; and, handing the keys back to the builder, he continued, "Here are the keys. They are yours. I had you build this house for yourself. You and your family are to have it as my gift."

In the years that followed, the carpenter never ceased to regret the way in which he cheated himself. "Had I only known," he would say to himself, "that I was building this house for myself..."

Building for the Future

A man was watching his eighty year old neighbor planting a small peach tree. He inquired of him, "You don't expect to eat peaches from that tree, do you?" The old man rested on his spade. He said, "No, at my age I know I won't. But all my life I have enjoyed peaches—never from a tree I planted myself. I'm just trying to pay the other fellows who planted the trees for me."

Laying Up Treasures in Heaven

Once there was a very rich man who dreamed he died and went to heaven. Saint Peter escorted him down a lovely street on which each house was magnificent. The rich man saw one house that was especially beautiful and asked who lived there. "That," said Saint Peter, "is the celestial home of your butler." "Well," the man said smiling, "if my butler gets a place like that, I certainly look forward to seeing what my new home will be like."

Soon they came to a very small street where the houses were tiny and unpretentious. "You will live in that hut," said Saint Peter, pointing his finger. "Me, live in that hovel!" "This is the best we can do for you," explained the saint. "You must understand that we only build your home up here with the material you send ahead while you are still on earth."

Change and Growth

One night a father decided that his son was now old enough to go out to the barn to feed the horses. The boy, however, told his father that he was afraid of the dark. The father stepped out onto the porch with the boy, lit a lantern, gave it to his son and asked him how far he could see as he held up the lantern.

"I can see halfway down the path," said the boy. The father directed his son to carry the lantern halfway down the path. When the boy reached that point, the father asked the boy how far he could see now. The boy called back to the father that he could see to the gate. The father urged the boy to walk to the gate, and, when the boy was at the gate, the father asked how far he could now see.

"I can see the barn," came the boy's reply. The father encouraged the boy to go to the barn and open the door. When the boy finally shouted back that he was at the barn and could see the horses, the father simply called, "Now feed the horses," and stepped into the house.

Possessions

In the last century, a tourist from America paid a visit to a renowned Polish rabbi, Hofetz Chaim. He was astonished to see that the rabbi's house was only a simple room filled with books, plus a table and a bench. "Rabbi," asked the tourist, "where is your furniture?" "Where is yours?" replied the rabbi. "Mine?" asked the puzzled American. "But I am only a visitor here. I'm only passing through." Said the rabbi, "So am I."

Remembering

According to legend, Zacchaeus arose early every morning and left his house. His wife, extremely curious at this strange behavior, decided to follow him one morning. She watched as her husband took a bucket to the well, filled it with water, and then walked out of the town gates. Zacchaeus stopped at a sycamore tree. There he set down the bucket and cleared away any debris which had accumulated at the foot of the tree. Having done this, he poured the water around the roots, caressed the trunk of the tree, and stood in seeming awe. At this point his wife came out of her hiding place and asked him what he was doing. Without hesitation Zacchaeus answered his wife's question by saying, "This is where I found Christ."

Discipline

The poet Samuel Taylor Coleridge was visited by an admirer one day. During the course of the conversation the subject somehow got around to children. "I believe," said the visitor, "that children should be given a free rein to think and act, and thus learn at an early age to make their own decisions. This is the only way they can grow into their full potential." Coleridge interrupted the man at this point. "I would like you to see my flower garden," said the poet, and he led the man outside. The visitor took one look and then exclaimed loudly, "Why, that is nothing but a yard full of weeds!" "It used to be filled with roses," said Coleridge, "but this year I thought I would let the garden grow as it willed without my tending to it. This is the result."

Example

In an old Chinese story a wise teacher asks his students to identify the most satisfying thing in life. There were many good answers given such as "a happy marriage," "good health," and "close friends." But the sage said that they all had failed to give the correct answer. "The most satisfying thing in life," he said, "is to see a child confidently walk down the road on his own after you have shown him the way to go."

Living Each Day

The story is told of a man who set out with a pilgrim's staff to find a certain saintly hermit to ask of him a question. When he found the hermit he said, "If you just had one day to live, how would you spend the day?"

The old hermit stroked his long white beard and answered, "Well, first I would say my morning prayer ... Afterward, I might fix a little tea and go out and weed the garden. Then I might go down the road to visit my neighbor John ... Then I might take a nap."

"Wait," the pilgrim interrupted, "that's the way you spend every day."

"Of course," replied the hermit. "Why should the last day be any different from the rest?"

Attentiveness

One evening a husband and wife were sitting on their back porch after dinner. They had both worked long and hard that day getting in the last of the hay. As many of us are accustomed to doing on a lazy, deliciously cool evening, the man fell asleep snoring in his rocker. As the woman continued relaxing, there happened one of those spectacular sunsets we would all like to photograph only to discover that the picture does no justice to the beauty. Thoroughly enjoying the sunset, the woman woke her husband so that he might share in the beauty. Saying to his wife, "It's just another sunset," the man went back to sleep.

Questioning

A father and his son were out walking one afternoon when the youngster asked how electricity went through the wires stretched between telephone poles. "I don't know," said the father. "I never knew much about electricity." A few blocks farther on the boy asked what caused lightning and thunder. "To tell the truth," said the father, "I never understood that myself." The boy continued to ask questions throughout their stroll, none of which the father could answer. Finally, as they were nearing their home, the boy said, "Dad, I hope you don't mind me asking so many questions." "Of course not," replied the father. "How else are you going to learn?"

Repentance

Two men once visited a holy man to ask his advice. "We have done wrong actions," they said, "and our consciences are troubled. Can you tell us what we must do so that we may be forgiven and feel clear of our guilt?"

"Tell me your wrong-doings, my sons," said the old man.

The first man said, "I have committed a great and grievous sin."

"What about you?" the holy man asked the second.

"Oh," he said, "I have done quite a number of wrong things, but they are all quite small and not at all important."

The holy man considered the matter for a while. "This is what you must do," he said at last. "Each of you must go and bring me a stone for each of his misdeeds."

Off the men went. Presently, the first man came back staggering with an enormous boulder, so heavy that he could hardly lift it, and with a groan he let it fall at the feet of the holy man. Then along came the second man, cheerfully carrying a bag of small pebbles. This he also laid at the feet of the saint.

"Now," said the holy man, "take all these stones and put them back where you found them." The first man shouldered his rock again, and staggered back to the place from which he had brought it. But the second man could only remember where a few of his pebbles had lain.

After some time, the second man came back and said that the task was too difficult. "You must know, my son, that sins are like these stones. If a man has committed a great sin, it lies heavy on his conscience; but if he is truly sorry, he is forgiven and the load is taken away. But if a man is constantly doing small things that are wrong, he does not feel any very great load of guilt, and so is not sorry and remains a sinner. So you see, it is as important to avoid little sins as big ones."

Repentance

The story is told of a first century rabbinic scholar who would tell his followers, "Repent one day before your death." "But how," they would ask, "does anyone know? One might die any day; it could be tomorrow, next week, or next year." "Then repent," he would say again, "one day before your death."

Repentance

An old story is told of a certain hermit who had lived for many years with a great reputation for sanctity and who began at length to entertain dangerous thoughts of self-complacency. Filled with these temptations, he was setting out one morning to visit a neighboring church when he beheld, seated on the banks of the river which flowed past his little cell, a poor man who appeared to be weeping bitterly.

On approaching him, the hermit perceived that the afflicted man was a notorious robber, the terror of the surrounding country. The hermit was about to retrace his steps when the man advanced to meet him, threw himself at his feet, confessed his crimes, and begged to know if he might ever hope for pardon.

The hermit, astonished and shocked at hearing the recital of so many enormous sins and comparing them with his own innocent and blameless life, began to swell with pride and in tones of indignation exclaimed, "Do you hope for pardon, you wicked sinner? Sooner shall roses bloom upon this dry staff than a just God will grant forgiveness to such sins as yours!"

So saying, he turned away, leaving the poor sinner on the brink of despair. The hermit had not proceeded far when the staff which he carried in his hand became rooted in the ground. He endeavored to pull it out, but it resisted all his efforts and became every moment more firmly seated in the soil. Then he beheld bud, and leaf, and flower sprouting forth until at last the dry stick was laden with beautiful roses; and at the same time he heard a voice whispering, "Sooner shall roses bloom on the barren staff than a good God will refuse mercy to the repenting sinner or grant it to the proud one."

At that, the hermit ran back to the sinner and made peace with him.

Forgiveness

From the Middle Ages comes this legend about a nun who claimed that she had had a vision of Christ. The bishop asked, "Sister, did you talk to him?" And she said, "Yes, I did." He continued, "If you have another vision, ask Christ this question: 'What was the bishop's great sin before he became a bishop?' " He knew that only God and his own confessor would know.

About three months later, the nun made an appointment to see the bishop. When she came in, he said, "Did you see our Lord again?" "Yes," she replied. "Did you ask him the question about my sin?" "Yes, I did." "And what did he say?" She smiled and answered, "The Lord said, 'I don't remember anymore.' "

The Stonecutter

There was once a stonecutter who was dissatisfied with his position in life. One day he passed a wealthy merchant's house, and through the open gateway, he saw many fine possessions and important visitors. "How powerful that merchant must be!" thought the stonecutter. He became very envious and wished that he could be like the merchant. Then he would no longer have to live the life of a mere stonecutter.

To his great surprise he suddenly became the merchant, enjoying more luxuries and power than he had ever dreamed of, envied and detested by those less wealthy than himself. But soon a high official passed by, carried in a sedan chair, accompanied by attendants, and escorted by soldiers beating gongs. Everyone, no matter how wealthy, had to bow low before the procession. "How powerful that official is!" he thought. "I wish *I* could be a high official!"

Then he became the high official, carried everywhere in his embroidered sedan chair. It was a hot summer day, and the official felt very uncomfortable in the sticky sedan chair. He looked up at the sun. It shone proudly in the sky, unaffected by his presence. "How powerful the sun is!" he thought. "I wish *I* could be the sun!"

Then he became the sun, shining down fiercely on everyone. But a huge black cloud moved between him and the earth, so that his light could no longer shine on everything below. "How powerful that storm cloud is!" he thought. "I wish that *I* could be a cloud!"

Then he became the cloud. But soon he found that he was being pushed away by some great force, and realized that it was the wind. "How powerful it is!" he thought. "I wish *I* could be the wind!"

Then he became the wind. But after a while, he ran up against something that would not move, no matter how forcefully he blew against it—a huge, towering stone. "How powerful that stone is!" he thought. "I wish *I* could be a stone!"

Then he became the stone, more powerful than anything on earth. But as he stood there, he heard the sound of a hammer pounding a chisel into solid rock, and he felt himself being changed. "What could be more powerful than I, the stone?" he thought. He looked down and saw far below him the figure of a stonecutter.

OBSTACLES ALONG THE WAY

Bad Habits

An old teacher was once taking a walk though a forest with a pupil by his side. The old man suddenly stopped and pointed to four plants close by his side. The first was just beginning to peep above the ground, the second had rooted itself pretty well into the earth, the third was a small shrub, while the fourth was a full-sized tree.

The tutor said to his young companion: "Pull up the first." The boy easily pulled it up with his fingers. "Now pull up the second." The youth obeyed, but found the task not so easy. "Now the third." The boy had to put forth all his strength, and was obliged to use both arms to uproot it. "And now," said the master, "try your hand at the fourth." But, lo, the trunk of the tall tree, grasped in the arms of the youth, hardly shook its leaves.

"This, my son, is just what happens with our bad habits. When they are young, we can cast them out more readily with the help of God; but when they are old, it is hard to uproot them, though we pray and struggle ever so sincerely."

Temptation

A rich man was trying to hire a chauffeur and he interviewed three men for the position. He pointed to a high cliff near his house and said, "Suppose you were driving me on the edge of that cliff. How close could you safely come?" One man said, "I could easily drive the car within six inches of the cliff and not think anything about it." Another man said, "I certainly could come within a foot without you having to worry at all." Finally, the third man applying for the job spoke up, "I wouldn't go anywhere near the edge of that cliff; I would stay at least six feet from the edge!" It was the third man who was hired for the job.

Locked into Our Own Thinking

On one occasion, the master escape artist Harry Houdini failed to make one of his spectacular escapes for which he was so famous. He was carefully searched by the jailers and then tied up with ropes, chains, and handcuffs. The jailers then closed the cell door and walked away. Houdini quickly, almost magically, freed himself from the shackles and then began working on the cell lock. But despite all his best efforts, the lock wouldn't open. Finally, frustrated and near exhaustion, he leaned against the door and it swung open so unexpectedly that he nearly fell into the corridor. The jailer forgot to lock the door.

The Total Picture

Once there was a town in which all the inhabitants were blind. A king with his entourage arrived one day with a mighty elephant which he used to impress his subjects. The people of the town were anxious to find out what an elephant was like and sent three of its blind members to investigate. Since none of them had ever seen an elephant, they groped sightlessly with their hands, gathering information by touching some part of the elephant.

When they returned to their fellow citizens, they were asked about the shape of the elephant. The man who had reached an ear said, "It is a large, round thing, wide and broad like a rug." The one who had felt the trunk said, "No, I have the real facts about it. It is a straight and narrow pipe, awful and destructive." The man who felt the leg said, "It is mighty and firm like a pillar." All were right in their own way, but all were blinded to the total picture.

Bad Example

When he was six years old, John was with his father when he was stopped for speeding. His father slipped the officer a twenty dollar bill with his license. "It's O.K., son.

Everyone does it." When John was nine years old he went shopping with his mother. The cashier accidently gave her too much change. As she slipped the extra money in her purse, she whispered to her son, "Everyone does it." When John was sixteen he landed his first summer job at the supermarket. One of his jobs was to put the overripe tomatoes at the bottom of the basket and the greener ones on the top. The boss told him, "It's good business."

When John was eighteen years old he went to college. One day he was approached by another student and asked if he wanted to buy some test answers. He did and was subsequently caught cheating and was sent home. His parents were very disappointed and said, "How could you have done such a dishonest thing? If there is anything the adult world cannot tolerate, it is a person who is dishonest."

Busyness

A farmer awoke one morning and looked out his window only to find that overnight a field of daffodils had sprung up about his home. "How beautiful!" he exclaimed. "I should like to stay and wander among the flowers, but I have to plow the north wheatfield today." When he returned that evening, the daffodils had withered and died.

The next day, the farmer saw two small sparrows perched on the branch outside his window. Their feathers were smooth and dark, and their song soared joyfully about him. "What beautiful music!" he sighed. "I will come and listen after I've milked the cows." But when he had returned, the birds had flown away.

The following day, the farmer awoke and heard the clatter of hooves on his front drive. He looked out the window and saw a great white stallion dancing and cavorting in the sunlight, inviting him to ride through the fields. "You are the most beautiful horse I have ever seen," he said. "I will return to ride off with you as soon as I have mended the south fence." When he returned, the stallion was gone.

Each morning for many years, the farmer witnessed some new wonder outside his window. But there was a farm to care for and he never found time to stop and share in these miracles.

Drawing Wrong Conclusions

There was an old woman who crossed the Brazilian frontier every day on a motor scooter with a sack of sand behind her. The customs officer eventually became suspicious and inquired, "What have you got in that sack?" "Only sand, sir," came the reply. The officer emptied the sack and, indeed, it contained nothing but sand. And so it went on for a month. One day, the officer said to the old woman, "I won't arrest you or say anything to the police, but just tell me: are you smuggling or not?" "Yes," she answered truthfully. "Well, what are you smuggling?" he pressed her. With a smile, she replied, "Scooters."

Gossip

A lady once went to confession to St. Philip Neri and confessed that she had been gossiping about others. As a penance St. Philip told her to go out and buy an unplucked fowl in the market place, and during her walk back she was to pull the feathers out one by one and scatter them along the way. Then she was to return to him and he would tell her what to do next. It seemed a strange penance, but she went off to the market place and did exactly what she was told, no doubt feeling a little foolish.

On her return, St. Philip praised her for her obedience. He said, "Now to complete your penance you must go back and pick up all the feathers." "But Father," the lady exclaimed, "you know that is impossible. The wind blew them away and I could never hope to capture them now." "Quite true," the saint replied. "Neither can you recall the damaging words about your neighbors which by this time have passed from mouth to mouth far beyond your reach. Be careful in the future and watch every word you utter."

Trying To Please Everyone

A father and his son took a donkey to the market. The man sat on the beast and the boy walked. People along the way said, "What a terrible thing: a big strong fellow sitting on the donkey's back while the youngster has to walk." So, the father dismounted and the son took his place. Soon onlookers remarked, "How terrible: the old man walking and the little boy sitting." At that, they both got on the donkey's back—only to hear others say, "How cruel: two people sitting on one little donkey." Off they got. But other bystanders commented, "How crazy: the donkey has nothing on his back and two people are walking." Finally, they both carried the donkey and they never did make it to the market.

Impatience

The great patriarch Abraham spent much of his life in the desert. One day he saw a stranger walking in the distance and he called out, inviting the traveler to dine with him and stay the night. The man readily agreed. But as Abraham was preparing to serve the meal, he learned that his guest was a fire-worshiper. He immediately threw him out of his tent without so much as a date to eat.

That night God appeared to Abraham in a dream and asked, "Why did you treat your guest as poorly as you did?" "Because he did not worship you, the one true God, my Lord," came the reply. The voice continued, "Abraham, Abraham, I have put up with that unbeliever for eighty years. Couldn't you have borne with him for one night?"

Gossip

It seems that several ministers from a small town were out fishing in a boat. As the fish weren't biting, they fell to talking. Since they had counseled their parishioners for many years that confession is good for the soul, they decided they would practice what they had been preaching. Each decided to confess his secret sin to the others.

The first said that his great fault was language; he still had trouble once in a while holding back improper words. The second minister admitted that his weakness was materialism; he was too fond of money and it was his first and main consideration in changing pastorates. The third preacher broke the news of an addiction to petty gambling on anything from golf to football.

The last minister, who was the helmsman on the small craft, had, by this time, turned the boat toward shore and had increased the speed. One of the confessors said, "What's the hurry? Besides you haven't made your confession." The minister replied, "Well, you see, my sin is gossip; and I just can't wait to get home."

Complaining

Monks, then as now, live very austere lives. But there was a time when they observed a strict rule of silence. In one monastery a monk was allowed to say only two words every five years, and those would be to the abbot. After his first five years of silence, one monk said, "Food cold." At the end of five more years he said, "Bed hard." Finally, after his fifteenth year in the monastery, he said, "I quit." "I'm not surprised," said the abbot. "All you've done is complain since you got here."

Procrastination

Three apprentice devils were preparing to come to earth to finish their apprenticeship. Satan, the Prince of Darkness, appeared before them and questioned them about their plans to tempt and ruin people.

The first said, "I will tell people that there is no God."

Satan answered, "You will deceive only a few that way because deep down people sense that there must be a God."

The second apprentice spoke, "I will tell them that there is no hell." "You will fool only a few that way," replied Satan, "because deep down people know one day they will have to answer for their misdeeds."

Finally, the third apprentice declared, "I will tell people that there is no hurry." With that, Satan laughed with delight and predicted, "You will ruin them by the millions."

Lying

A preacher saw a group of small boys sitting in a circle with a dog in the middle. He asked what they were doing. One boy said, "We're just telling lies, and the one who tells the biggest one gets to keep the dog." The preacher said, "Why, I'm shocked. When I was a little boy, I never even thought of telling a lie." The little boy said, "Give him the dog, fellas. He's the winner."

Misreading the Bible

Once there was a man who wanted to know God's will on a particular matter. He took his Bible, opened it at random, and dropped his index finger onto the page, assuming that the verse on which it landed would tell him what to do. But much to his chagrin, his finger fell on Matthew 27:5 which reports that Judas went out and hanged himself. The man thought he had better try it again. This time his finger came to rest on the admonition of Luke 10:37, "Go and do likewise." When he followed the same method a third time, his finger fell on these words in John 13:27, "Be quick about what you are to do."

Apathy

His companions were making fun of the ragged, barefoot boy. "You're a Christian," they taunted him. "If God loves you, why doesn't he take better care of you? Why doesn't he tell someone to give you a pair of shoes?" The boy seemed puzzled for a moment. Then, with tears in his eyes, he replied, "I think he does tell people. But they're not listening."

No Heart

The time was now. Jesus decided he was ready to choose his twelve apostles. Just advertising in the newspapers didn't seem thorough enough. So Jesus decided to hold an Olympics from which the twelve would be chosen. The people came from all over. The competition was fierce. Jesus had to judge all the events.

First came the prayer event. People had practiced and it showed in the speed with which they could recite the words. Some articulated the words with utmost precision. Some used big impressive words. Still others expressed lofty ideas. But when it came time for a winner to be selected, Jesus chose none. There didn't seem to be any heart in their prayers. They were just words.

Second came the worship event. These contestants too had done their homework. Some wore beautiful garments. Some used lots of incense. Some emphasized music. Others incorporated gestures. But again, when it was selection time, there was no winner. There didn't seem to be any heart in worship. It was too showy.

Third came the teaching event. This was a prepared group. Some came with elaborate posters. Some came with long, well-ordered talks. Some came with video-cassette recorders. Others came with their small groups to demonstrate process. Again, no winners. There was no heart in their teaching. The methods seemed more important.

So the Olympics ended. No winners, no apostles. Exhausted after this long exasperating ordeal, Jesus went down to the lake to cool off and relax. Then the miracle happened. He saw people fishing. Now there were some people who put their hearts into what they were about! So he chose them.

Indifference

A young minister went to his first church with eager enthusiasm. To his disappointment, he found the worship services poorly attended and the spiritual life of the congregation at low ebb. He called from house to house seeking renewed interest, but several people said the church was so dead that they did not care to attend. He discussed the situation with his church board and they agreed that the criticism was probably justified.

The pastor announced that since the church was considered dead, he would conduct its funeral the following Sunday. The church was crowded that day. In front of the pulpit was a coffin. The minister eulogized the deceased. He told how much the church had accomplished in the past and expressed his sorrow over its untimely demise. Then he invited the congregation to go forward and view the corpse. One by one the people looked into the casket; each was amazed to see his own face reflected from a mirror in the bottom of the coffin. Many were shocked and indignant, but then each member began to realize that his or her own spiritual indifference was the reason the church was dead.

Prejudice

A Chinese man and a Jewish man are eating lunch together. Suddenly, without warning, the Jew gets up, walks over to the Chinese fellow and smashes him in the mouth, sending him sprawling. The Chinese man picks himself up, rubs his jaw and asks, "What did you do that for?"

And the answer comes back, "For Pearl Harbor!"

His response is total astonishment—"Pearl Harbor? I didn't have anything to do with Pearl Harbor. It was the Japanese who bombed Pearl Harbor."

The Jew responds, "Chinese, Taiwanese, Japanese—they're all the same to me."

With that they both sit down again, and before too long the Chinese man gets up, walks over to the Jew, and sends him flying with a hard slap to the jaw. The Jew yells out, "What did you do that for?"

And the answer comes back, "The Titanic!"

"The Titanic? Why, I didn't have anything to do with the Titanic!"

Thereupon the Chinese man replies, "Goldberg, Feinberg, Iceberg—they're all the same to me."

Failure To Appreciate

An elderly woman died and left her coin collection to her favorite niece. At first the woman was excited about the inheritance until she found that her aunt had only thirty-five coins in the collection. One morning, many months later, she threw the coins into a bag and went off to work.

During her lunch hour, she stopped at a coin shop to determine the value of the coins. When the dealer looked at the coins, he gasped in disbelief. These coins were extremely rare and valuable. When he informed her of her great wealth, the niece admitted that she suspected the coins were of value, but she never dreamed they were that valuable. With the help of the shopkeeper, the woman was able to sell the coins for a large sum of money.

Loss of Faith

A playful five year old boy watched his father smoking a pipe and blowing smoke rings. He ran across the room to where his father sat, playfully cupped some of the smoke in his hands, and ran off to the corner of the room with his treasure. He opened his hands and, to his surprise, found no smoke in them. He immediately ran back to where his father sat smoking, cupped some more smoke in his hand, and slowly moved toward the corner as though he were carrying eggs. Again, he found no smoke when he opened his hands. He looked confused for a moment and then ran off to play another game.

Frustration

The story is told of a time when Saint Teresa of Avila was planning to take a trip. Before she left, she prayed that she might travel safely. But her travel was marred by various mishaps and accidents. When she finally arrived at her destination, she turned to God, not to pray, but to complain about how poorly God had protected her during the trip. "But, Teresa," the Lord reportedly answered, "you know this is how I treat all my friends." "If that is so," she responded, "then it's no wonder you have so few of them!"

Practice What You Know

There was a young book salesman who was assigned to a rural area. Seeing a farmer seated in a rocking chair on his front porch, the young man approached him with all the zeal of a newly trained salesman. "Sir," he said, "I have here a book that will tell you how to farm ten times better than you are doing now." The farmer continued to rock. After a few moments he stopped, looked at the young man, and said, "Son, I don't need your book. I already know how to farm ten times better than I am doing now."

Forgetting God

A spider built his web in a barn, high among the rafters, where he started by spinning a long, thin thread attached to the end of one of the beams. With this thread still attached to him, the spider jumped off the beam and spun out more thread on the way down, until he reached the place he planned as the center of his web. From the center, he then spun out other threads like the spokes of a wheel, attaching each end of them to the walls and other places. Finally he had an exquisitely made web that helped him catch many fine fat flies. But he grew fat, and lazy, and vain.

One day, while admiring the web he had spun, he noticed the long fine thread he had first spun from the top beam and said, "I wonder what that is for? I can't imagine why I ever put it there; it doesn't catch any flies." And so on a sudden impulse he broke it. But as a result the whole wonderful web collapsed. The spider had forgotten that the one thread—the link to the strongest beam above—supported the whole web.

Inconsistency

A priest was accosted by a mugger while walking down a dark alley. The thief demanded that he hand over his wallet. As the priest opened his coat to reach for his wallet, the would-be mugger saw the collar and realized he was robbing a priest. He immediately apologized and said, "Forget it, Father. Keep your money. I had no idea you were a priest." Both nervous and relieved, the priest took out a cigarette and offered one to the stranger. "No thank you," the robber said. "I gave up smoking for Lent."

Lip Service

A naive villager, born and raised in an obscure rural environment, came to the big city for the first time and obtained lodging at an inn. Awakened in the middle of the night by the loud beating of drums, he inquired drowsily, "What's all this about?" Informed that a fire had broken out and the drum beating was the city's fire alarm, he turned over and went back to sleep.

On his return home, he reported to the village authorities, "They have a wonderful system in the big city; when a fire breaks out the people beat their drums and before long the fire burns out." All excited, they ordered a supply of drums and distributed them to the population. When a fire broke out later, there was a deafening explosion of beating of drums, and, while the people waited expectantly for the flames to subside, a number of their homes burned to the ground.

A sophisticated visitor passing through that village, when told the reason for the ear-splitting din, made fun of the simplistic natives. "Idiots! Do you think a fire can be put out by beating drums? They only sound the alarm for the people to wake up and take measures to extinguish the fire."

Not Living Up to the Name

A soldier in the army of Alexander the Great was brought before the great world-conqueror for a court-martial. When the emperor had listened to the charges and the evidence, he turned to the soldier facing condemnation and said, "What is your name?"

"Alexander," was the reply.

Again the emperor questioned, "What is your name?"

And the second time the soldier answered, "Alexander."

With a cry of rage, the emperor roared, "What is your name?" And when the soldier answered a third time, "Alexander," the great general angrily replied, "You say your name is Alexander? You are found guilty of your crime as charged and now you must pay the penalty. Either change your conduct or change your name, for no man can bear the name of Alexander, my name, and do the things you have done."

Know Thyself

A prosperous young Wall Street broker met, fell in love with, and was frequently seen escorting about town a rising actress of gentility and dignity. He wanted to marry her, but being a cautious man he decided that before proposing matrimony he should have a private investigating agency check her background and present activities. After all, he reminded himself, I have both a growing fortune and my reputation to protect against a marital misadventure. The Wall Streeter requested that the agency was not to reveal to the investigator the identity of the client requesting a report on the actress.

In due time the investigator's report was sent to the broker. It said that the actress had an unblemished past and a spotless reputation, and that her friends and associates were of the best repute. "The only shadow," added the report, "is that currently she is often seen around town in the company of a young broker of dubious business practices and principles."

Splinter in One's Eye

A man once stole a piece of food and was ordered by the king to be hanged. When asked if he had any last words, the thief replied, "Know, O king, that I can plant an apple seed in the ground and it will grow and bear fruit overnight. It is a secret that my father taught me and I thought it would be a pity if it died with me."

A time was appointed the following day for planting the seed. The thief dug a hole and said, "This seed can only be planted by someone who has never stolen or taken anything which did not belong to him. Being a thief, I cannot, of course, do it."

The king asked his prime minister to plant the seed. But he hesitated and said, "Your majesty, when I was young, I recall keeping an article that did not belong to me. I cannot plant the seed."

The treasurer, when told to plant the seed, begged the king's pardon, saying that he may have cheated someone out of some money. The king, in his turn, recalled that once he took and kept a precious object belonging to his father.

The thief turned to them and said, "You are all mighty and powerful persons. You are not in want of anything, yet you cannot plant the seed. Yet I, who stole a little food to stay alive, am to be hanged." The king, pleased with the man's wisdom, pardoned him.

Resolutions

Late one December an elementary school principal said to his teachers, "Let's all write out New Year's resolutions about how we can be better teachers and I'll put them on the staff bulletin board." The teachers agreed, and when the resolutions were posted, they all gathered around the bulletin board to read them.

One of the young teachers suddenly went into a fit of anger. "He didn't put up my resolution. It was one of the first ones in. He doesn't care about me. That just shows what it's like around here." On and on she ranted and raved.

The principal, who overheard this from his office, was mortified. He hadn't meant to exclude her resolution. Quickly rummaging through the papers on his desk, he found it and immediately went to the bulletin board to put it up. The resolution read, "I resolve not to let little things upset me anymore."

Judging Others

Two Buddhist monks on their way to the monastery found an exceedingly beautiful woman at the river bank. Like them, she wished to cross the river, but the water was too high. So one of the monks lifted her on his back and carried her across. The fellow monk was thoroughly scandalized. For two full hours he berated him on his negligence in keeping the holy rule: Had he forgotten that he was a monk? How dare he touch a woman—and, more, actually carry her across the river? And what would people say? Had he not brought their holy religion into disrepute? And so on and so forth. The offending monk patiently listened to the never-ending sermon. Finally, he broke in with, "Brother, I dropped the woman at the river. Are you still carrying her?"

Greed

There is an old Russian folktale about a peasant couple who after each evening meal say, "If only we had enough land, then we would be happy." As the story progresses, the couple come into a little more land, but the meal always ends with the same wish. In time they acquire a great deal of land and become wealthy landowners.

One day a neighboring Tartar who has more land than they do comes to share their table. When the meal ends with the usual wish, the Tartar asks, "How much land is enough?" The peasant, now a gentleman, responds that all the land he could walk around in a single day would be enough. The Tartar tells him that he may walk his land and have all that his feet touch providing he makes a full circle.

The man sets out at dawn and walks and jogs all day, always widening his circle to gain a little more land. Come sunset, he can see his wife and the Tartar at the end point of his journey. Instead of heading straight for them, he decides to make one more circle to encompass the magnificent home of the Tartar. Just as the sun sets, he reaches his wife's arms. Victorious, he laughs—then dies; his overworked heart has failed him.

He is buried the next day. Once again the Tartar asks how much land is enough, then answers his own question: "Why, that is easy! No one needs more than a plot three feet by six. Our friend finally has enough land."

Trials

A powerful king, ruler of many domains, was in a position of such magnificence that wise men were his mere employees. And yet one day he felt himself confused and called the sages to him. He said, "I do not know the cause, but something impels me to seek a certain ring, one that will enable me to stabilize my state. I must have such a ring. And this ring must be one which, when I am unhappy, will make me joyful. At the same time, if I am happy and look upon it, I must be made sad."

Then the wise men consulted each other, threw themselves into deep contemplation, and finally came to a decision as to the nature of this ring which would suit their king. The ring which they devised was one upon which was inscribed the legend: "This, too, will pass."

Suffering

A Chinese peasant lived in a small village with his wife and teenage son. Through much hard work, he was able to buy a mare. "You are so fortunate to have such a fine mare," said the villagers. "I am only a human, and only the gods know of good fortune," replied the old man. One day the mare ran away. "How unfortunate," said the villagers. "I accept the judgment of the gods," said the man. Some days later, the mare returned, followed by a fine stallion. "Now you have two fine horses. You are indeed a lucky man!" cried the townspeople. "I know that only the gods know," said the old man.

The old man's son decided that he would break the stallion so that it would be able to help with the work on the farm; he was thrown off and broke his leg in six places, making him limp very badly. "Alas, now your beloved son is lame for life," said the villagers. "Only the gods know why," said the old man. Weeks passed, and a company of soldiers came to the village and took away all the young men to fight in the army—all but the lame young man. The villagers gathered at the old man's house to congratulate him on his good fortune at being able to keep his son. "You were right," they said. "Only the gods *do* know."

Suffering

An artist went to visit a dear friend. When he arrived, she was weeping. When asked why, she showed him a handkerchief of exquisite beauty which had great sentimental value, but which had been ruined by a drop of indelible ink. The artist asked her to let him have the handkerchief, which he returned to her several days later. When she opened the package she could hardly believe her eyes. The artist, using the inkblot as a base, had drawn a design of great beauty with Indian ink. Now it was more beautiful than ever.

Suffering

Once there was a man who wanted to have a lion tattooed on his back. He went to a tattoo artist and told him what he wanted. But as soon as he felt the first few pricks, the man began to moan and groan. "You are killing me. What part of the lion are you marking?" "I am just doing the tail now," said the artist. "Then leave the tail out," howled the other.

So the artist started again. And again the client could not stand the pricks from the needle. "What part of the lion is it this time," he cried, "for I cannot stand the pain?" "This time," said the tattooist, "it is the lion's ear." "Let us have a lion without an ear," gasped the patient.

So the tattooist tried again. No sooner had the needle entered his skin than the victim squirmed again. "Which part of the lion is it this time?" "This is the lion's stomach," wearily answered the artist. "I don't want a lion with a stomach," said the other man.

Exasperated and distraught, the tattoo artist stood a while. Then he threw down his needle and cried, "A lion without a head, with no tail, without a stomach? Who could draw such a thing? Even God did not!"

Attendance at Sunday Worship

There was a Catholic man who would always say to his wife on Sunday mornings, "You can go to Mass for both of us." One night he dreamed that he and his wife died and came together to heaven's gate. St. Peter asked, "You are Mr. and Mrs. Smith?" The couple both nodded their heads. "Well, Mrs. Smith can come in for both of you!" declared the saint.

Faith Must Be Lived

A rabbi and a soapmaker went for a walk together. The soapmaker said, "What good is religion? Look at all the trouble and misery of the world after thousands of years of teaching about goodness, truth, and peace—after all the prayers, sermons and teachings. If religion is good and true, why should this be?"

The rabbi said nothing. They continued walking until he noticed a child playing in the gutter. Then the rabbi said, "Look at that child. You say that soap makes people clean, but see the dirt on that youngster. Of what good is soap? With all the soap in the world, the child is still filthy. I wonder how effective soap is after all."

The soapmaker protested and said, "But, Rabbi, soap can't do any good unless it is used."

"Exactly," replied the rabbi. "So it is with Judaism or any other religion. It is ineffective unless it is applied and used."

Bad Preaching

When the minister ended the long, dry sermon, he asked for the board of deacons to remain for a few minutes after the service. Among those who stayed was a man the preacher didn't recognize. "Sir," he said politely, "I asked that only the board remain." "Then that includes me," the man said. "I was never more bored in my life."

Living in the Future

Aaron was a fisherman who lived on the banks of a river. Walking home with his eyes half-closed one evening after a hard day's toil, he was dreaming of what he would do when he became rich. Suddenly, his foot struck against a leather pouch filled with what appeared to him small stones. Absentmindedly, he picked up the pouch and began throwing the pebbles into the water. "When I am rich," he said to himself, "I'll have a large house." And he threw a stone. He threw another stone and thought, "I'll have servants and wine and rich food." This went on until only one stone was left. As Aaron held it in his hand, a ray of light caught it and made it sparkle. He realized then that it was a valuable gem, and that he had been throwing away the real riches in his hand while he dreamed idly of unreal riches in the future.

The Unforgivable Sin

A rich man entered a village and called all the poor people together in the town square. He told them that he wanted to share his wealth with them by giving each person enough money to help begin a new life.

Some of the poor people rushed forward, grateful to the rich man and eager to accept his great gift. Those who knew this man were not surprised, since they realized how generous he was and that he asked for little in return. Others of the village, however, said that there were some strings attached to this gift. No one gives away something without hoping for something in return. They accused the rich man of using his wealth for the sake of controlling others and they refused to take any of his wealth.

When the rich man left that village, some of the people were ready to begin a new life, while others, who mistrusted the rich man, had condemned themselves to a life of suffering in poverty and hunger.

DESTINY AND THE WAY

The Journey's Goal

A salt doll journeyed for thousands of miles over land until it finally came to the sea. It was fascinated by this strange moving mass, quite unlike anything it had seen before. "Who are you?" said the salt doll to the sea. The sea smilingly replied, "Come and see." So the doll waded into the sea. The further it walked in the sea the more it dissolved until there was only very little of it left. Before the last bit dissolved, the doll exclaimed in wonder, "Now I know who I am!"

The Stream

A stream, from its source in the far-off mountains, passing through every kind and description of countryside, at last reached the sands of the desert. Just as it had crossed every other barrier, the stream tried to cross this one, but found that as fast as it ran into the sand, its waters disappeared. It was convinced, however, that its destiny was to cross the desert, and yet there was no way. Now a hidden voice, coming from the desert itself, whispered, "The wind crosses the desert and so can the stream."

The stream objected that it was dashing itself against the sand only to be absorbed, that the wind could fly, and this was why it could cross the desert. Said the desert: "By hurling in your own accustomed way you cannot get across. You will either disappear or become a marsh. You must allow the wind to carry you over to your destination."

But how can this happen? "By allowing yourself to be absorbed by the wind." This idea was not acceptable to the stream. After all, it had never been absorbed before. It did not want to lose its individuality. And, once having lost it, how was one to know that it could ever be regained?

"The wind," said the sand, "performs this function. It

takes up the water, carries it over the desert, and then lets it fall again. Falling as rain, the water again becomes a river."

"How can I know this is true?"

"It is so, and if you do not believe it, you cannot become more than a quagmire, and even that could take many, many years; and it certainly is not the same as a stream."

"But can I not remain the same stream that I am today?"

"You cannot in either case remain so," the whisper said. "Your essential part is carried away and forms a stream again. You are called what you are even today because you do not know which part of you is the essential one."

When he heard this, certain echoes began to arise in the thoughts of the stream. Dimly, he remembered a state in which he or some part of him had been held in the arms of the wind. He also remembered—or did he?—that this was the real thing, not necessarily the obvious thing to do.

And the stream raised his vapor into the welcoming arms of the wind which gently and easily bore it upward and along, letting it fall softly as soon as they reached the roof of a mountain many, many miles away. And because he had had his doubts, the stream was able to remember and record more strongly in his mind the details of the experience. He reflected, "Yes, now I have learned my true identity."

And Then What?

A young student came to Saint Philip Neri one day and told him he was to study law. "What a happy man I am. I am going to study and become a learned man."

"And then what?" asked Father Philip.

"Then I shall become a great lawyer and win fame."

"And then what?"

"Then I shall become very rich and build a beautiful home for myself."

"And then what?"

"Then I shall marry and live in comfort to a ripe old age."

"Francis, then what?"

Francis knew no further answer. After some thought, he said, "Then, like everybody else, I shall die."

"And then what, Francis?"

The young man was disturbed, but he answered gravely, "Then I shall await to learn what judgment will come upon me." Here he stopped. He could not answer further. This question made him change all his plans for the future.

Preparing for Death

One day a court jester said something so foolish that the king, handing him a staff, said to him, "Take this and keep it until you find a bigger fool than yourself."

Some years later the king was very ill and lay on his deathbed. The king, addressing those gathered around his bed, said, "I am about to leave you. I am going on a very long journey, and I shall not return to this place; so I have called you to say goodbye."

Then the jester stepped forward and addressed the king, saying, "Your majesty, may I ask you a question? When you journeyed abroad visiting your people, staying with your nobles, or paying diplomatic visits to other kings, your heralds and servants always went before you making preparations for you. May I ask what preparations your majesty has made for this journey you are about to take?"

"Alas," he said, "I have made no preparations."

"Then," said the jester, "take this staff with you, for now I have found a bigger fool than myself."

No Need To Fear Death

There is a story about a famous Japanese samurai swordsman who ran a school. One day, a young man came to him for lessons. As was the samurai's custom, he began with a contest in which he pitted his own swordsmanship against that of his pupil. With great fervor he attacked the pupil, but each time he would strike or thrust, the young man would skillfully deflect the blow. When the contest was over, the samurai congratulated the young man and asked him under whom he had studied. The young man replied that he had no formal training in the sword. How was it that he fought so skillfully, the samurai asked. "I have learned not to fear death," the young man replied.

Death and Eternal Life

In the year 627 the monk Paulinus visited King Edwin in northern England to persuade him to accept Christianity. He hesitated and summoned his advisors. At the meeting, one of them stood up and said, "Your majesty, when you sit at table with your lords and vassels, in the winter when the fire burns warm and bright on the hearth and the storm is howling outside, bringing snow and rain, it happens all of a sudden that a little bird flies into the hall. It comes in one door and flies out through the other. For the few moments that it is inside the hall, it does not feel the cold, but as soon as it leaves your sight, it returns to the dark of winter. It seems to me that the life of man is much the same. We do not know what went before and we do not know what follows. If this new doctrine can speak to us surely of these things, it is well for us to follow it."

Mourning

A little girl was sent to the store with specific instructions from her mother to come directly home after her purchases. She was more than two hours coming home, much to the distress of her anxious mother. "Where have you been?" scolded the mother.

"I'm sorry, Mommy. I know I am late, but Jane broke her doll and I had to stop and help her fix it."

"And how could you help her fix that broken doll?"

In her precious, childlike manner the girl responded, "I really couldn't, but I sat down with her and helped her cry."

The Bottom Side

A little girl was walking along beside her father on an evening stroll. She kept looking up at the stars. She was fascinated by them, but she wasn't talking about it. Finally her father asked her what she was thinking about and she answered, "If the bottom side of heaven is so beautiful, how wonderful the other side must be. That's where Mommy is and I know how much she loves beautiful places." The child was walking knee-deep in stardust and in that moment she helped her dad take hold of the hand of God.

Heaven

There was a man whose one consuming passion was to go to heaven. Finally, he died and did go there. An angel took him by the hand and showed him the beautiful sights, the majestic mountains, lovely flowers, gorgeous sunsets, little children playing in the streets. He exclaimed, "Isn't heaven wonderful?" But the angel said, "This isn't heaven; this is the world in which you lived but which you never saw."

Heaven and Hell

A righteous man was permitted by God to attain foreknowledge of the world to come. In a celestial palace he was ushered into a large room where he saw people seated at a banquet table. The table was laden with the most delectible foods, but not a morsel had been touched. The man gazed in wonder at the people seated at the table because they were emaciated with hunger and they moaned constantly for food even though it was in front of them.

"If they are hungry, why is it that they don't partake of the food that is before them?" asked the man of his heavenly guide. "They cannot feed themselves," said the guide. "If you will notice, each one has his arm strapped straight, so that no matter how he tries, he cannot get the food into his mouth." "Truly, this is hell," said the righteous man as they left the hall.

The heavenly attendant escorted him across the hall into another room, and the man observed another table equally as beautiful and laden with delicacies and choice foods. Here he noticed that those seated around the table were well-fed, happy, and joyous. To his amazement, he saw that these people, too, had their arms strapped straight. Turning to his guide he asked in perplexity, "How is it that they are so well fed, seeing they are unable to feed themselves?"

"Behold," said the guide. The righteous man looked and saw that each one was feeding the other. "In truth," he exclaimed, "this is really heaven!" "In truth it is," agreed the attendant. "As you can see, the difference between hell and heaven is a matter of cooperation and serving one's fellow."

Death

When Moses had to inform his brother Aaron of Aaron's impending death, he sat down with him and read the narrative of the creation of the world in the Book of Genesis. As they read of the creation of each day, Moses exclaimed, "How beautiful and good was the creation of this day!"

But when they reached the description of the creation of Adam, Moses said, "I don't know what to say about the creation of man. How can I call it beautiful and good when the end of man is death?" Aaron quickly replied, "We must resign ourselves to the will of God." And that answer gave Moses an opening to tell Aaron about his approaching death.

Footprints

A man dreamed he died and went to heaven and there was met by Jesus. The man had lived a long Christian life, but it had not been without some times of great trial and tribulation as well as those times of joy and victory. As he met with Christ, the man was given a panoramic review of his life—all the highlights and low periods. In the review of his life one of the things that continued throughout were his footsteps along the sands of time.

The man noticed that at those times in his life when it had really been rough there was only one set of footprints—not two as in the good times. The man turned to the Lord and said, "Lord, I don't understand. You promised to be with me always. But when I look back now, I see that in those really rough times there was only one set of footprints. Lord, why did you leave me then?"

The Lord looked at him, smiled, and said, "Leave you? I didn't leave you at all. Dear friend, if you look at the footprints carefully, you'll notice they are a little deeper than the others. Those were the times I was carrying you."

Making the End Glorious

A wise old woman happened to be a pianist who had taught many students over the years. Invariably, when she prepared her pupils for recitals, she would have them practice the conclusions over and over again. Invariably the students would begin to grumble because of the constant repetition of the last few measures of music. When one would voice their complaints, the wise teacher would always answer, "You can make a mistake in the beginning or you can make a mistake in the middle. The people will forget it if you make the ending glorious."

Acknowledgements

This book would not have been possible without the cooperation and generous permission of a number of writers and publishers. To them I express my heartfelt gratitude. Many of the books and magazines cited below include a rich variety of stories for preaching and teaching for those who wish to augment their own collection of stories.

Regrettably, there are a number of stories included in the collection for which I am unable to give proper credit. Some are from other preachers I have heard while others were simply given to me by people who know my love for stories. When the authors become known, proper credit will be given in any future editions of this book. Others are from books and publishers which are out of print or no longer in business.

Desire

Pulpit Resource, 121 Maono Pl., Honolulu, HI, 96821, vol. 9, no. 1, p. 46.

Many Ways

Meyer Levin, *Classic Hasidic Tales,* New York: Penguin Books, © 1975, p. 47f. Reprinted by permission of the author and the author's agents, Scott Meredith Literary Agency, Inc., 845 Third Avenue, New York, NY, 10022.

Searching

James Field, CFX, "The Paschal Fast: Good Friday and Beyond." *Assembly* 6:4 (1980) :85. Published by the Notre

Dame Center for Pastoral Liturgy, Notre Dame, IN, 46556.

Cease Struggling

Walter B. Knight, *Knight's Master Book of New Illustrations,* Grand Rapids: Wm. B. Eerdman's Publ. Co., 1982, p. 592.

Prayer Is the Key

Reprinted with permission from *Twelve and One-Half Keys* by Rev. Edward M. Hays (1981: Forest of Peace Books, Inc., Easton, KS, 66020), p. 9f.

Close to Home

From *Finding God in Everyday Life* by Rev. Kevin Coughlin, © 1981 by Kevin Coughlin. Used by permission of Paulist Press, p. 7.

God Is Waiting To Be Found

Taken from *Rabbinic Wisdom and Jewish Values* by William Silverman, revised edition © 1971 by the Union of American Hebrew Congregations, p. 21.

Answering the Call of Christ

Taken from *Simple Sermons from the Gospel of Matthew,* by W. Herschel Ford. Copyright 1963 by Zondervan Publishing House, p. 27. Used by permission.

Look Together

Parables, Etc. (Saratoga Press, James S. Hewett, Editor and Publisher), 14200 Victor Place, Saratoga, CA, 95070, vol. 4, no. 1, p. 3.

Respond Now

F. H. Drinkwater, *Catechism Stories,* Westminster: Newman Press, 1948, p. 12.

Finding Grace at the Center

Source unknown.

So Simple It Is Difficult

See 2 Kings 5:1–14.

Letting Go

This story is reprinted with permission from *Storytelling: Imagination and Faith,* copyright 1984 by William J. Bausch (paper, $7.95) published by Twenty-Third Publications, Mystic, CT, 06355, p. 127f.

What We Can Be

This excerpt from *Emphasis,* A Preaching Journal for the Parish Pastor, C.S.S. Publishing Co., Lima, OH 45804, vol. 13, no. 9, p. 18.

Conversion

Walter B. Knight, *Knight's Master Book of New Illustrations,* Grand Rapids: Wm. B. Eerdman's Publ. Co., 1982, p. 16.

Leap of Faith

Source unknown.

Empty Yourself

Adapted from an ancient Zen tale.

Awareness

From *Scripture Comes Alive* Homily Service, published by Alt Publishing Co., P.O. Box 400, Green Bay, WI, 54305.

Discipleship

From Phil Barnhart, *Seasonings for Sermons,* Lima, OH: C.S.S. Publishing Company, © 1980, p. 91. Used with permission.

Church

Aesop's Fables.

Church

Reprinted by permission of *Celebration: A Creative Worship Service,* P.O. Box 281, Kansas City, MO, 64141 (Dec. 9, 1985).

Evangelize

James F. Colaianni, *Sunday Sermons Treasury of Illustrations,* Pleasantville: Voicings Publications, 1982, p. 150.

Share the Good News

James F. Colaianni *Sunday Sermons Treasury of Illustrations,* Pleasantville: Voicings Publications, 1982, p. 149.

Holiness

Taken from *Rabbinic Wisdom and Jewish Values* by William Silverman, revised edition © 1971 by the Union of American Hebrew Congregations, p. 74.

Faith

Parables, Etc. (Saratoga Press, James S. Hewett, Editor and Publisher), 14200 Victor Place, Saratoga, CA, 95070, vol. 2, no. 8, p. 7.

Faith

Parables, Etc. (Saratoga Press, James S. Hewett, Editor and Publisher), 14200 Victor Place, Saratoga, CA, 95070, vol. 2, no. 11, p. 2.

Trust in God

Pittsburgh Post-Gazette, as told by Joe Browne, June 6, 1983.

Hope

Nathan Ausubel, ed., *A Treasury of Jewish Folklore,* New York: Crown Publishers, 1948, p. 570.

Love One Another

Reprinted from *Three Minutes a Day,* © The Christophers, 1949, p. 228.

Love of Neighbor

Parables, Etc. (Saratoga Press, James S. Hewett, Editor and Publisher), 14200 Victor Place, Saratoga, CA, 95070, vol. 4, no. 3, p. 5.

Charity

Reprinted by permission of *Celebration: A Creative Worship Service,* P.O. Box 281, Kansas City, MO, 64141, Sept. 12, 1976.

Service

Source unknown.

Give Thanks

© John Tonne, *Five Minute Homilies on the Gospels of Cycles A,B,C,* St. John Church—Pilsen, Marion, KS, 66861, p. 97.

What Prayer Is Not For

Selection taken from *Weekday Homily Helps,* February 15, 1982, published by St. Anthony Messenger Press, 1615 Republic St., Cincinnati, OH, 45210. Used with permission.

Prayer

Source unknown.

Prayer

Excerpt from *Under the Fig Tree* by William Breault, S.J., copyright 1980 by Ave Maria Press, Notre Dame, IN, 64556, p. 55f, is used by permission of the publisher. All rights reserved.

A Vision for the Future

Pulpit Resource (Glendon Harris, Publisher and Editor), 121 Maono Pl., Honolulu, HI 96821, vol. 10, no. 1, p. 29.

Combating Evil

Taken from *Rabbinic Wisdom and Jewish Values* by William Silverman, revised edition © 1971 by the Union of American Hebrew Congregations, p. 55.

How To Change the World

"Bayazid Breaks the Rule" from *Song of the Bird* by Anthony de Mello, S.J. Copyright © 1982 by Anthony J. de Mello, S.J. Reprinted by permission of Doubleday & Company, Inc.

Gentleness

Reprinted from *Quotes and Anecdotes* by Anthony P. Castle, © 1979, p. 57f. Published by Kevin Mayhew, Ltd., 55 Leigh Road, Leigh-on-Sea, Essex SS91JP, England.

Co-Partner with God

Taken from *Rabbinic Wisdom and Jewish Values* by William Silverman, revised edition © 1971 by the Union of American Hebrew Congregations, p. 207.

Building for the Future

Taken from *Rabbinic Wisdom and Jewish Values* by William Silverman, revised edition © 1971 by the Union of American Hebrew Congregations, p. 207f.

Building for the Future

Parables, Etc. (Saratoga Press, James S. Hewett, Editor and Publisher), 14200 Victor Place, Saratoga, CA, 95070, vol. 4, no. 7, p. 2.

Laying Up Treasures in Heaven

Ralph Woods, *Wellsprings of Wisdom,* C.R. Gibson Co., Knight St., Norwalk, Conn. 06856, p. 66. Used by permission of the author.

Change and Growth

In His Light, by Rev. William Anderson, © 1979, reprinted with permission of Wm. C. Brown Company Publishers, p. 2.

Possessions

Source unknown.

Remembering

What Is A Christian? by A. Leonard Griffith, Abingdon Press, 1962, P.O. Box 801, Nashville, Tenn., 37202, p. 18.

Discipline

Quote (A. L. Kirkpatrick, Publisher), 405 Sussex Place, 148 International Blvd., Atlanta, GA, 30303, vol. 84, no. 13, p. 296.

Example

Source unknown.

Living Each Day

From *Along the Water's Edge* by Daniel Juniper, © 1972 by The Missionary Society of St. Paul the Apostle in the State of New York. Used by permission of the Paulist Press.

Attentiveness

Paul Wharton.

Questioning

Pulpit Resource, 121 Maono Pl., Honolulu, HI, 96821, vol. 9, no. 3, p. 6.

Repentance

Reprinted from *Quotes and Anecdotes* by Anthony P. Castle, © 1979. Published by Kevin Mayhew Ltd., 55 Leigh Rd., Leigh-on-Sea, Essex SS91JP, England.

Repentance

Source unknown.

Repentance

Henry Fehren, *U. S. Catholic,* reprinted with permission, published by Claretian Publications, 221 West Madison St., Chicago, IL, 60606, vol. 49, no. 5, p. 40.

Forgiveness

This excerpt from *Emphasis*—A Preaching Journal for the Parish Pastor, C.S.S. Publishing Co., Lima, OH, vol. 13, no. 5, p. 30.

The Stonecutter

From *The Tao of Pooh,* © 1982 by Benjamin Hoff. Reprinted by permission of the publisher, E.P. Dutton, a division of New American Library, p. 118ff.

Bad Habits

Walter B. Knight, *Knight's Master Book of New Illustrations,* Grand Rapids: Wm. B. Eerdman's Publ. Co., 1982, p. 274.

Temptation

Source unknown.

Locked into Our Own Thinking

Source unknown.

The Total Picture

From *Tales of the Dervishes,* © 1967 by Idries Shah. Reprinted by permission of the publisher, E.P. Dutton, a division of New American Library, p. 25.

Bad Example

From *Scripture Comes Alive* Homily Service, published by Alt Publishing Co., P.O. Box 400, Green Bay, WI, 54305, 12/30/84.

Busyness

Source unknown.

Drawing Wrong Conclusions

Source unknown.

Gossip

F. H. Drinkwater, *Catechism Stories,* Westminister: Newman Press, 1948, p. 237.

Trying To Please Everyone

This excerpt from *Emphasis*—A Preaching Journal for the Parish Pastor, C.S.S. Publishing Co., Lima, Ohio, vol. 14, no. 4, p. 4.

Impatience

The Talmud.

Gossip

Pulpit Resource, 121 Maono Pl., Honolulu, HI, 96821, vol. 9, no. 4, p. 30f.

Complaining

Source unknown.

Procrastination

Adapted from William Barclay, *Gospel of Matthew, vol. 2,* Philadelphia: The Westminster Press, 1975, p. 317.

Lying

Quote (A.L. Kirkpatrick, Publisher), 405 Sussex Place, 148 International Blvd., Atlanta, GA, 30303, vol. 84, no. 10, p. 224.

Misreading the Bible

Source unknown.

Apathy

James Keller, Reprinted from *Three Minutes a Day,* © The Christophers, p. 298.

No Heart

John R. Schmitz, "Getting Caught," *Service,* 1984, vol. 1, p. 63f. Copyright 1984 by the Missionary Society of St. Paul the Apostle, in the State of New York. Used by permission.

Indifference

Source unknown.

Prejudice

Parables, Etc. (Saratoga Press, James S. Hewett, Editor and Publisher), 14200 Victor Place, Saratoga, CA, 95070, vol. 2, no. 11, p. 4.

Failure To Appreciate

Journeying in His Light by Rev. William Anderson, © 1983. Reprinted with permission of Wm. C. Brown Company Publishers, p. 127.

Loss of Faith

In His Light by Rev. William Anderson, © 1979. Reprinted with permission of Wm. C. Brown Company Publishers, p. 106.

Frustration

Source unknown.

Practice What You Know

Source unknown.

Forgetting God

Ralph Woods, *Wellsprings of Wisdom,* C. R. Gibson Co., Knight St., Norwalk, Conn., 06856.

Inconsistency

Source unknown.

Lip Service

Pulpit Resource, 121 Maono Pl., Honolulu, HI, 96821, vol. 9, no. 1, p. 20.

Not Living Up to the Name

Walter B. Knight, *Knight's Master Book of New Illustrations,* Grand Rapids: Wm. B. Eerdman's Publ. Co., 1982, p. 750.

Know Thyself

Ralph Woods, *Wellsprings of Wisdom,* C. R. Gibson Co., Knight St., Norwalk, Conn., 06856. Used by permission of the author.

Splinter in One's Eye

Source unknown.

Resolutions

James F. Colaianni, *Sunday Sermons Treasury of Illustrations,* Pleasantville: Voicings Publications, 1982, p. 85.

Judging Others

"The Monk and the Woman" from *Song of the Bird,* by Anthony de Mello, S.J. Copyright 1982 by Anthony de Mello, S.J. Reprinted by permission of Doubleday and Company, Inc.

Greed

Source unknown.

Trials

From *The Way of the Sufi,* copyright 1968 by Idries Shah. Reprinted by permission of the publisher, E.P. Dutton, a division of New American Library, p. 74.

Suffering

Martin Buxbaun. *Quote,* vol. 84, no. 3, p. 62.

Suffering

Parables, Etc. (Saratoga Press, James S. Hewett, Editor and Publisher), 14200 Victor Place, Saratoga, CA, 95070, vol. 1, no. 5, p. 2f.

Suffering

From *The Way of the Sufi,* copyright © 1968 by Idries Shah. Reprinted by permission of the publisher, E.P. Dutton, a division of New American Library, p. 248f.

Attendance at Sunday Worship

F. H. Drinkwater, *Catechism Stories,* Westminster: Newman Press, 1948, p. 255.

Faith Must Be Lived

Taken from *Rabbinic Wisdom and Jewish Values* by William Silverman, revised edition © 1971 by the Union of American Hebrew Congregations, p. 127.

Bad Preaching

Quote (A. L. Kirkpatrick, Publisher), 405 Sussex Place, 148 International Blvd., Atlanta, GA, 30303, vol. 84, no. 24, p. 505.

Living in the Future

Reprinted from *Three Minutes a Day,* © The Christophers, p. 295.

The Unforgivable Sin

William Anderson (used with permission).

The Journey's Goal

"The Salt Doll" from *Song of the Bird,* by Anthony de Mello S.J. Copyright 1982 by Anthony de Mello, S.J. Reprinted by permission of Doubleday & Co., Inc., p. 124.

The Stream

From *Tales of The Dervishes,* copyright © 1967 by Idries Shah. Reprinted by permission of the publisher, E.P. Dutton, a division of New American Library, p. 23f.

And Then What?

Lawrence Lovasik, *Catechism in Stories,* Milwaukee: The Bruce Publishing Co., 1956, p. 103.

Preparing for Death

Reprinted from *Quotes and Anecdotes,* by Anthony P. Castle, © 1979. Published by Kevin Mayhew Ltd., 55 Leigh Road, Leigh-on-Sea, Essex SS91JP, England.

No Need To Fear Death

Reprinted by permission of *Celebration: A Creative Worship Service,* P.O. Box 281, Kansas City, MO, 64141, Nov. 2, 1985.

Death and Eternal Life

Source unknown.

Mourning

J. Wallace Hamilton as quoted by James Christensen, *Difficult Funeral Services,* Old Tappan, N.J., 07675, Fleming H. Revell Co., 1985, p. 101.

The Bottom Side

Source unknown.

Heaven

Source unknown.

Heaven and Hell

Taken from *Rabbinic Wisdom and Jewish Values* by William Silverman, revised edition © 1971 by the Union of American Hebrew Congregations, p. 180f.

Death

Voices of Wisdom: Jewish Ideals and Ethics for Everyday Living, edited by Francine Klagsbrun, New York: Pantheon Books, A Division of Random House, Inc., © 1980, p. 233.

Footprints

Anonymous.

Making the End Glorious

Source unknown.

Topical Index

Please note that the letter following a page number refers to either the first, second, or third TITLED *story on a page. For example, if you were looking for a story about apathy, one could be found either in the third story on page 49 or in the first story on page 50.*

Index for Preachers

With the caution that many of these stories can be used in different ways, an index is presented here as a suggestion to preachers for when certain stories might be used. The letter following the page indicates whether the story is the first, second, or third TITLE *on the page. For example, if you were looking for a story for the Feast of the Ascension, the first and second titled stories on page 22 would be appropriate.*